POETRY FOR THE EYES

Novasel Landscape Lighting

3 Sylvan Road South
Westport, CT 06880
1 800 201-1408
203 454-4800

- Elegant, understated landscape illumination for your home

- One day installation available

- Security Lighting

 Please call for additional information

Martha's December

TUESDAY	WEDNESDAY	THURSDAY	FRIDAY	SATURDAY	SUNDAY
		1 Move outdoor gardens indoors	**2**	**3** Scrub north face of house with Borax	**4** Touch up trim in Yemen apartment
5	**6** Weed indoor gardens	**7** 8:30 a.m. "This Day" show appearance w/ Bryant & Katie	**8**	**9** 4:00 a.m. Montauk L.I. Catch giant tuna for dinner	**10** Neuter pets & barnyard animals	**11** Change glue in all 55 glue guns
12 Bake, bake, bake	**13** Sell, sell, sell	**14** 8:30 a.m. "This Day" show appearance/grab Bryant under desk	**15**	**16** Recipe-testing dinner for staff of "Chutzpa!" magazine	**17** Make planters from used tractor trailer tires for NJ relatives	**18** Make napkins, tablecloth, candles & toothpicks for dinner guests
19 Gild runover chicks for Christmas ornaments	**20** Realign branches on tree & glue	**21** 8:30 a.m. "This Day" show appearance/ exchange glares with Bryant	**22** Stalk, shoot, gut, bleed & defeather turkeys/baste overnight	**23**	**24** Spank Manuel & rest of staff	**25** Build creche/ play Mary

CHRISTMAS |
| **26** Start planning Christmas 2000 | **27** | **28** Call police to remove relatives from grounds | **29** Design line of aluminum foil panties | **30** Harvest ice from pond for drinks | **31** Invite Manuel in for cocktails

NEW YEAR'S EVE | |

2

Martha's
January

MONDAY	TUESDAY	WEDNESDAY	THURSDAY	FRIDAY	SATURDAY	SUNDAY
1 Pick up green cards for Manuel & staff NEW YEAR'S DAY	**2** Climb Mt. Everest/gather oxygen for making water	**3** Work on script for "Martha," the movie	**4**	**5** Sleep for half an hour	**6**	**7** Re-glaze greenhouse
8 Stencil driveway	**9** Move chicken coops two feet to the right	**10** Detail lawnmowers & weedwackers	**11** Organize leather closet	**12**	**13** Work on script for "Martha," the musical	**14** Stencil street
15 Harvest betelnut crop	**16** Scrape & paint Westport, Southampton and Vermont homes	**17** Order 100 varieties of apple saplings	**18** Prune prune trees	**19** Force forsythia, hyacinth, quince & Manuel	**20** Stencil turnpike exit ramp	**21** Aluminum-side trailer home behind main house
22 Harvest ewe bark for sale to Sloan-Kettering	**23**	**24** Sue Martha's Vineyard over name	**25** Gather wild rice in Minnesota for chicken soup	**26** Put down Appaloosa's for glue	**27** Meet with Norman Mailer on "Martha," the book	**28** Surf Bonzai Pipeline
29 Consult with Pope at Vatican (possible stencil op)	**30** Run with bulls at Pamplona	**31** Breakfast at Tiffany's/lunch at K-Mart				

Breakfast on Mt. Everest

A LETTER FROM MARTHA

FOR YEARS I HAVE SHARED WITH READERS MANY OF THE SIMPLER HOME PROJECTS THAT HAVE brought me a sense of accomplishment and satisfaction. None of the projects were actually *doable*, but that isn't the point. The point is that I'm tired of hearing from women who say, "Martha, I just can't live up to your expectations." What most women fail to understand is that perfection in the home doesn't happen suddenly in middle age. It begins in childhood.

Growing up in a large Polish household in New Jersey, by the age of four I was hosting afternoon teas for my dolls, and by six arranging birthday parties using my brother and the neighborhood kids as staff. It was an incident in the 4th grade, however, that was to influence profoundly how I view entertaining. Three girls I admired were standing together on the playground before class. As I passed I heard one of them say, "How many Poles does it take to give a dinner party?" "How many?" the other girls answered, giggling with anticipation. "None," went the punchline, "what's a dinner party?" Everyone laughed. At home later that day, I tied up my dolls, spanked my brother and fired the neighborhood help. From that moment on, I decided I would do everything — and I mean *everything* — myself, and I would do it perfectly.

Lacking my history, readers can only share in some of the even simpler, easier tasks I demonstrate in the following pages. You won't be able to do any of these either. Yet by simply *attempting* to do what I do, you will come that much closer to knowing what it is like to be me. And that should be enough for any woman.

Martha Stuart

contents

CONTINUED ON PAGE 7

GINGERBREAD CASTLE

Dear Martha:

Last Christmas season, I began constructing the gingerbread replica of Windsor Castle according to architectural plans found in your book, "Casual Holiday Entertaining." Now, nearing completion and finding that not only have my house guests left, but also my husband and children (whom, I understand, have since been placed in a more nurturing home environment), I have just one question: Do the caramelized sugar windows have to open or can they just look as if they do?

— Waiting To Hear
Akron, Ohio

Dear Waiting:
Of course they have to open.
Lazy bitch.

Dear Martha:

I am writing to invite you to be the next Ambassador to Toomeekistan, the former Soviet province in the Northwestern region. We are hoping that you will accept this position, as the population is in desperate need of strict homekeeping standards.

As you will learn from the enclosed briefing papers, Toomeekistan is in an almost unbearably tasteless state. Its citizens are alternately unruly and comatose, motivated solely by pilferage and vodka. If you accept this challenging assignment to transform and redecorate the country, you will be expected to yell, scold, berate and occasionally beat the population, with a complete disregard for their feelings. I eagerly await your reply.

Cordially,
— Christopher Warren
U.S. Secretary of State
Washington, D.C.

Dear Martha:

My boyfriend tells me I should try to be more like you. But after working in the garden all day, I look and smell like some kind of compost queen and can never get my hair to stick out in a fright-wig the way yours does. Please help.

— Martin S.

Dear Martin:
Just relax and try to be
natural.

RECIPE ADVICE

Dear Martha:

Although I no longer have access to kitchen facilities, I have maintained a healthy interest in your magazine, which I read every month in the library here. I consider myself an exceptional cook and I am particularly drawn to the recipes and the "What to have for dinner" section. I like picturing what your suggestions would look like as they simmer on the stove in my old apartment and the puzzled looks on my former neighbors' faces as they cautiously sniff the air, trying to guess.

Which brings me to a question about your heartier dishes. I was just wondering, as a general rule, can the beef in your recipes be replaced by any other type of meat?

— J. Dahmer
#DE32188976
Milwaukee, Wisconsin

Dear J.:
One of the great things about my recipes is that they can be adapted to whatever ingredients you may have at your disposal. So let your imagination run wild, J. Dahmer, and dig in!

Dear Ms. Stuart:

I am outraged by your repeated suggestions that women enslave themselves to demeaning household project chores and self-defeating ideals of wifely perfection.

Continued on page 63

contents

IS MARTHA STUART LIVING?

Producers	Tom Connor Jim Downey
Photographer	J. Barry O'Rourke
Writers	Tom Connor Jim Downey Joy Haenlein Elizabeth Hilts Bob Morris Meredith Anthony & Alison Power
Model	Suzy Pemberton The Johnston Agency/Norwalk, Connecticut
Legal Representation	Scott Johnson/Greenwich, Connecticut Alan Neigher/Westport, Connecticut John Rapoport/New York, New York
Food Stylist	John Carafoli
Computer Layout & Production Manager	Christine Rooney RIS, Incorporated/Norwalk, Connecticut
Computer Manipulations	Toby Welles Design Core/Redding, Connecticut
Business Advisor	Lisa E. Grenadier
Spiritual Advisor	Linda Downey
Fashion Styling	ESG Styling
Country Kitchen	Gallery of Kitchens & Baths/Westport, Connecticut
Garden Map	Tom Muckenstrom/Monroe, Connecticut
Water Label	Jack Robson/Westport, Connecticut
China & Table Setting	Abbey Richmond/Fairfield, Connecticut
Christmas Trees	Louis Bacchiocchi Woodwise Consulting/West Haven, Connecticut & The Connecticut Audubon Society
Dried Flowers	Anabelle Green Cannon Crossing/Wilton, Connecticut
Leather	Phillip Kohan R&S Leather Sportswear/Bridgeport, Connecticut
Stacked Logs	Mimi Lipton from "Stacking Wood" (Thames & Hudson, 1993)
Tools	Thanks to Glen & Nancy at Village Hardware/ Southport, Connecticut; Bob Kelly of The Jelliff Corp./Southport; and Ron Schooler, Bill Berkow and Darryl Manning

Many thanks to Scott & Liz Johnson, Alan Neigher, Beth McPadden, Kate Coleman, Mary Connor Moffitt & Anne Moffitt, Michael Grenadier, George & Del Grenadier, Bob Rieb, Toby Welles, Jack Robson, Chance & Debra Browne, Darryl Manning, Harvey & Bonnie Brooks, Patty Robinson, Marge Thompson, Susan McDonald, Rick Wolff, Gene Brissie, Jim Charlton, Deb Werksman & Hysteria Magazine, Debbie Gore, Scott Bondlow, Maggie Ellsworth, Christine Loomis, Peggy Kamen, and Tom and Getrude Connor.

Special thanks to Lisa & Jack Connor, Linda Downey & Jacey Haskell, Carol & Barry O'Rourke, and to John & Peter Featherston.

FIRST EDITION

ISBN 0-06-095182-6

95 96 97 98 99 10 9 8 7 6 5 4 3 2 1

HarperPerennial
A Division of HarperCollinsPublishers

CONTRIBUTORS

J. BARRY O'ROURKE'S photographs have appeared on the covers of more than 200 major national and international magazines. A New York-based advertising and editorial photographer for more than 30 years, he was a staff photographer for Playboy in the '60s, and is the author of the best-selling photo book, "How to Photograph Beautiful Women." He is also part-owner of The Stock Market, a photo stock house run for photographers in Manhattan, and currently produces videos and commercials.

JOHN CARAFOLI is a chef and food stylist in Boston and New York who has won many awards for his work. Before studying food with Madeleine Kamman, he served as creative director and art director for advertising agencies and magazines. Today, he teaches cooking at the Boston University Culinary Institute, Peter Kump's New York Cooking School and at Bed & Breakfast of Sagamore on Cape Cod, which he owns and operates. Carafoli is the author of "Food Photography and Styling" (Amphoto, 1992).

BOB MORRIS, who wrote the piece about guest lists in our "Entertaining" section in this issue, writes "The Night" column for The New York Times "Style" section. He also contributes to "Details" magazine. Morris coined the phrase, "the dominatrix of domesticity" (see centerfold).

JOY HAENLEIN is a staff reporter for The Stamford Advocate and Greenwich Times in Fairfield, County, Connecticut. She has also written for The Detroit News and worked as a stringer for The New York Times. For this issue, Haenlein wrote "How to Dominate Tag Sales" and contributed to "Recollecting" and "Letters to Martha". Her ambition: "To re-do the bottom of my swimming pool with copies of this magazine."

MEREDITH ANTHONY & ALISON POWER are contributing editors of Hysteria magazine. They wrote the "Gardening" article in this issue. "We consider ourselves feminist/humorists writing about feminist topics," says Anthony, "although we deviate from that from time-to-time and actually will write about anything for money." The two are also co-authors of "101 Reasons Why We're Doomed: A Cynic's Guide to What's Left of the Future" (Avon Books).

TOBY WELLES, whose computer manipulations appear in this issue, is head of Design Core, an industrial design and computer animation studio in Redding, Connecticut. In addition to manipulating images in this issue, Welles admits to manipulating his friends. His work has been published in Computer Graphics World and Computer Artist, and shown at the Silvermine Galleries, among other places.

ELIZABETH HILTS is the acting editor of two alternative newspapers, The Fairfield Weekly in Fairfield County, Connecticut, and The Westchester County Weekly in New York. She contributed to "Letters To Martha" and to the "Gardening" article in this issue. Hilts, who is the author of "Getting In Touch With Your Inner Bitch" (Hysteria Publications, 1994), notes that before beginning her career as an editor and free-lance writer, she was a devoted homemaker for 12 years. "The fruit of that labor was a divorce and minimal earning power," she says. "Now, I'm the authority on bitches."

90-grain bread

Bake bread at least once a week, bake lots of bread, bake an unreasonable number of loaves of bread. And when you bake that bread, make it with grain, lots of grain, lots of different grains, as many grains as you can possibly cram in the breadpan. Become obsessed about the number of grains a single loaf of bread can contain. Bread is a good thing

things

trout holding pond

Fresh trout makes for a wonderful dinner, but who has the time to go flyfishing on the river before the guests arrive? Instead, catch and release trout into a holding pond on the property. Cut ice for centerpiece ice sculptures or chop into cubes for drinks.

stenciled driveway

Art, we know, often imitates life. So that when some chicks wandered across the driveway from the Maison de Poulet and were accidentally run over by a Range Rover (honestly, I didn't see them), I cried, then was immediately inspired to immortalize the chicks by tracing their outline and stenciling the dead-chick pattern, left, on the black-

top. Take a recently-deceased pet, any pet. After it has been sufficiently flattened, use a piece of chalk to draw its form on the driveway or other surface. Then lay tracing paper over the chalk form, re-trace with a No. 9 pencil and transfer the new outline to stiff cardboard. Cut out the pattern. Repeat up one side of the driveway and down the other. Continue on street.

well-stacked logs

Anyone can fell a tree, haul it home, chop it up, split the logs and toss them onto a pile. But a well-designed log pile is truly a thing of beauty. Try stacking wood in a variety of ways, starting with the three patterns shown above. Try not to use the logs. The idea is to impress others, not warm the house. If the winter is cold and you must use them, take logs from the least successful and attractive pile first.

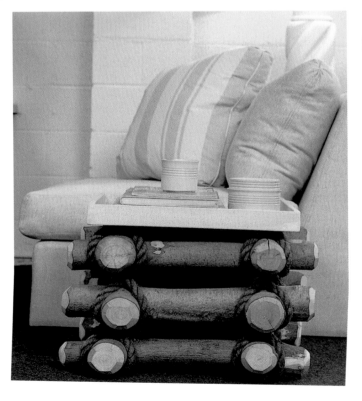

log table

When winter finally wanes and you find yourself down to the last few logs, don't burn them, turn them into end tables that will remind you of the season past long after the last snows have melted. If it has been a mild winter and there's plenty of firewood left over, make chairs, sofas, beds, cabinets and kitchen counters out of logs to keep busy. Re-side your house with logs.

Making Water
from scratch

I WAS AT A PARTY THE OTHER DAY WHERE WATER WAS SERVED. I WAS QUITE thirsty and looked forward to a refreshing drink, but when one of the help set down a lovely-looking pitcher of chilled water I was shocked. There was no bouquet, no sense of history. Where did this particular water come from, I had to wonder? What glacier, mountain stream, underground aquifer? To be perfectly frank, none of the above. This water had no personality. This water was dead.

It was not the first time I'd been served dead water, but I resolved that it would be the last. If I were to eliminate imperfect water from my world, I would have to make water myself.

In theory, the necessary ingredients are quite simple, really: one part oxygen to two parts hydrogen. But in practice, I had difficulty finding a local supplier who could provide me with enough quality hydrogen. After several weeks of investigative work, however, I found a wonderful old gentleman in Germany who apparently had had experience during World War II making what he called "heavy water." It was from him that I procured some really lovely vintage hydrogen.

In addition to having the right elements, the utensils and mixing bowls used in the preparation of this basic drink also are extremely important. I find that a Yak butter bowl given to me by some sherpa pals in Tibet imparts a rich, earthy flavor. Zebra wood beakers, carved from trees I clear-cut myself in the Brazilian rainforest, give the water the right woody overtones. And a 200-year-old horsehide beer pouch from a relative in Poland adds an Old World aftertaste. Once you've carefully separated the hydrogen in a total vacuum, add the oxygen one molecule at a time. Let the mixture sit overnight at .027 degrees Kelvin. The next morning, you will have given birth to a clear and complex water.

In the beginning I brewed a few drops at a time, but I quickly learned that to produce a full bottle of superlative water, one need simply multiply my recipe by 60 billion (*see "Recipes"*).

ATTENTION TO DETAIL COMES IN HANDY IN MY WORLD. LIVING PERFECTLY DEMANDS vigilance and hard work. Gilded pumpkins, after all, don't grow on vines. It's not even enough to perform household tasks perfectly. Only the perfectly perfect will do.

Sleepless in Westport

But the bedcorners are perfect

Which brings me to an often neglected but extremely important detail of the home: bedcorners.

It always saddens me to visit a home and uncover an imperfectly-made bed — the linens in disarray, the corners soft and indecisive-looking — for I know that the homeowner is missing the deep, visceral pleasure that comes from turning a bedcorner so sharply you could shave your legs with it if you had to.

When preparing to make a bed, there are three separate axes that must be taken into account: pitch, yaw and roll. Using a previously calibrated spirit-level, tune the sleeping surface to sea-level, thus locking in the yaw. Roll adjustments can be set with large surgical calipers using the bed frame/box-spring clearances as parameters. Pitch is critical for a subliminal esthetic appeal to sleepers and can best be tweaked by suspending a plumb bob from a point above the bed, then snapping a line to each of the corners.

If you have followed my instructions, you are now ready for the linen preparation. I soak rotating sets of 700-point, South Sea Island, pima-cotton sheets overnight in a mixture of starch derived from imported Irish new potatoes and a light, glue-based fixative from one of my herd of Appaloosas, bred exclusively for this purpose. When dry, these sheets will hold a crease all night long.

Now, using a protractor, steel T-square and a 12,000-watt professional heat gun, construct four precise, 90-degree hospital corners that will be the envy of any registered nurse in the world.

You might not sleep particularly well, since corners this perfect require that you lie flat and stay still. Your family and houseguests may not recognize your efforts. You may even begin to doubt the importance of a well-disciplined bed. And, naturally, tomorrow morning you will have to repeat the procedure.

But I never said this would be easy. I never said it would be fun. All I said was that it must be done.

Clean Sweep

There are really only five ways to sweep a floor

LIKE ANYTHING ELSE IN LIFE, THE CHOICE OF A BROOM AND A SWEEPING style must be given careful and thorough consideration. I have found that one should only use a broom manufactured in the same region and period as the floor being swept.

The mellow, striated grain of a circa early 18th-century random-width pine board, for instance, seems to recognize the straw from a broom with the same lineage and thus will yield its hold on dirt more easily. A recently-manufactured surface, on the other hand, such as any of the new coverings flooding the American market from China, respond well to any fine bamboo-shafted broom with natural cotton or hemp bindings.

But the perfect broom doesn't guarantee a clean sweep. It is also necessary to adjust one's sweeping style and grip to the broom and floor at hand. Under no circumstances should you ever mix stroke styles; the accidental mix of a French Twist start with a Native American "Jay" stroke finish, for instance, can flick a fine coating of dust right up onto the lip of the shoe molding or wainscoting.

Try beginning with the American Standard stroke. This great, basic sweeping stroke begins with your legs firmly planted, weight evenly distributed, and left and right big toes at 10 and 2 o'clock respectively. Remember that in sweeping, as in life, follow-through is everything.

As you feel the power travel up through your legs, turn your hips in the direction you wish to propel the dirt. Keep your head down. Picture in your mind where you want the dust, dirt and hairballs to land. At the very end of the sweep, gently lift the tip of the broom. This will place topspin on the upper layer of dirt, keeping it low to the floor, exactly where you want it.

German Dust Stifle

American Standard

There are hundreds of sweeping styles being used around the world today. Some are lovely to look at but inefficient. Some get the job done but they do so with very little style. These five classic grips are at once graceful and pragmatic. Each one is an excellent example of good dirt control and lyrical, balletic movement.

English Reverse

Eastern European Backspin

French Twist

Gardening

Martha's Garden

Martha's Vineyard

East Prune Orchard

Neutering Shed

Staff Barracks

Pheasant Run

Quintuple-Dug Vegetable Garden

High-speed Bakery with En-croutery

Fast-food Delivery Access Road

Child Care Containment Maze

Mower Detailing Shop

Parent's Guest
Quarters

Guilding
Studio

Arugula Salad Garden

Leather
Shop

Catering Barn

Scallion Patch

...batoir

Maison
de
mierde

Geothermal
Cappuccino
Steam Valve

...scargot Pond

Mined-Croquet Lawn

Control
Central

Main Driveway

Wild and hearty, ornamental grasses grow freely in vacant lots and highway medians, provide shelter in fall and early winter and, when lightly steamed, make an intriguing sidedish.

Homeless
but not
Gardenless

MANY YEARS AGO, WHEN MY DAUGHTER FIRST VISITED NEW YORK'S METROPOLITAN MUSEUM of Art with her class, she appreciated the French Impressionists and Rembrandt's use of light. But what most impressed her was a woman outside the Museum who was laden with shopping bags and "falling down like you do, Mommy, after you've spent all day baking babas au rhum." My daughter said the woman was playing house on a park bench. When I told her that the bench probably was the woman's home, she thought for a moment, then said, "But where's her garden?"

Homelessness is one of the most critical social issues of our day, and one to which I'm most sensitive. But homelessness needn't mean gardenless. Whether in the city or the suburbs, it is possible for the habitat-challenged to turn a vacant lot and some richly-composited garbage into a showcase of sorts.

First, you must determine the zone in which you subsist. If you are fortunate enough to be home-less in California, for instance, your gardening options are virtually unlimited. Those of us who face the climactic challenges of Connecticut, the Hamptons or Times Square, however, must adapt without being daunted. If I can coax four-inch blooms from my Madame Defarge hybrid pink antique rosebush on unpredictable Long Island, stunning hybrids can surely be cultivated on Manhattan's Lower East Side. And if I can produce sumptuous ornamental grasses and Queen Anne Lace on my rocky farm in Westport, others can grow them equally well in the vacant lots and median strips on the West Side.

What if your soil is mostly sand, clay or concrete? A portable herb and lettuce garden can be fashioned from a discarded shopping cart lined with a Hefty bag that has outworn its use as a winter coat. Fill with good, friable soil from a street divider (I like Park Ave.). By being completely mobile, you will enjoy the privilege of being able to wheel your moveable feast about the town, following the sun (something I envy).

For those with some sort of address, a trellis fashioned from domestic lager cans will support morning glories, wisteria and other flowering vines, double as a windscreen in harsher weather and, in most states, can always be redeemed for cash. I find that empty Chinese takeout cartons (the best are those from Luchows or Wu Wong's) make for excellent urban pots for seedlings or transplants.Or gather up Queen Anne's Lace and other natural lot covers with brightly-colored ribbon — the yellow and black tapes used at crime scenes make a statement.

Dirt

1. This is a wonderful driveway mixture I've developed. It's designed to have a very satisfying, high-fidelity, crunching sound underfoot. The tone that reaches your ears can be adjusted by gently grinding down the shape of each individual stone. For more treble and a crisper, more antiseptic sound, leave more sharp edges, for more bass and a more mellow over all sound, grind till almost smooth. An added benefit is that, since this mix has pumice stone in it, it actually cleans the soles of your shoes on the way into the house.

2. Here is a lovely little dirt I use as the topmost layer in plant pots. It is a spectacular light reflector due to the addition of Madagascar quartz crystals. Proper placement near a sunny window will allow you to aim, focus and color the light in a room as you weave the sun's rays through the crystals. After some practice, I learned how to throw a wash of filtered, equalized light, indistinguishable from that at Arles in the French countryside. Finally, your Impressionist paintings can be viewed in the same light they were painted in.

3. A classic antique dirt that I got under license from Thomas Jefferson's estate at Monticello. The curator there made me privy to a little secret. Jefferson was given the dirt (which is from the mushroom cellar at the Versailles Palace) as a birthday present from the nation of France and there is a persistent rumor that the Sun King himself, Louis the XIV, stole it from the burial chamber in the great pyramid at Cheops. I realize that one can never really own a dirt this important and that I am only its temporary steward, but it does make a wonderful pedigreed grout between my pantry floorboards.

4. This is dirt I found near the shore in northern Oregon. It has the unique ability to actually absorb and retain the smell of the salt air at the oceanside and then release this rich aroma on command at a later date. The best method I have found for freeing the fragrance is to grind it between two counter-rotating 800-pound millstones. When sprinkled around at any party, your guests will soon be wondering when the tide is going to come in.

5. Here is a lovely combination of dirt and oil I discovered when I was consulted on methods for tidying up the EXXON-VALDEZ spill. After removing any seagull feathers or otter fur, it's ideal for rubbing on new gardening clothing to simulate the rich patina that usually comes with years of use.

6. This is topsoil from the oldest, continuously operated farm in the world. It was in the AHK-BARR valley in central Egypt. The last of 61 generations of tenant farmers died recently and a pal brought me 14 tons. There is no dirt in the world like this for growing Papyrus, from which I can make anything from a boat to an envelope.

Handmade Condoms

A fitting gift for the '90s

ONE OF MY EARLIEST CHILD-HOOD MEMORIES IS OF MOTHER FASHIONING CHASTITY BELTS from used farm machinery for men and women guests alike. But on those rare dinner occasions when lamb was served, Aunt Katrina would make prophylactics out of the sheep's intestinal lining, then test them by filling the balloon-like

membranes with water and dropping them from a second floor window on the heads of arriving guests. How her laughter filled the house!

I first experimented with condoms made from sheep's intestines on my honeymoon. That early effort was less than perfect, but by dawn I had crafted a good enough version to satisfy, at least for the time being, my quest for the best.

More recently, when one of the sheep accidentally died the day before a dinner party, I seized the opportunity to make a gift for my guests that is as practical as it is romantic, and one utterly fitting for the '90s.

After stalking, slaying, bleeding and eviscerating the animal (see "Raising Livestock," August/September '90 issue), rinse the long lining from the animal's lower intestine in tap water and let sit overnight in a vat of Virgin olive oil and K–Y jelly. Pick garden vegetables of varying shapes and sizes the next morning, then mold the prophylactics around them. Seal with your glue gun and roll while still warm.

For a special treat, try decorating the tips or bases of the condoms with romantic designs: hearts, a winged Cupid with bow and arrow, a mistletoe leaf or my initials. You also may want to leave a little of the casing, as I do, for a nice, fresh lamb kielbasa.

Perfect Fit

1. After selecting the appropriate fruit or vegetable for the guest you have in mind (I prefer zucchini), and after wrapping the sheep's membrane around it, seal with your glue gun. A little extra glue at the tip, by the way, never hurt anyone. **2.** Roll lining down the length of the vegetable, gluing along the underseam as you go. **3.** Apply a romantic or fanciful stencil, at this stage or while on your guest, at the base of the condom and reroll. **4.** Combine leftover membrane and lamb meat for a sidedish of Kielbasa (see "Recipes").

Getting In Touch With Your Inner Bitch

BY
ELIZABETH HILTS

For the woman who wants to laugh out loud and speak her mind,
Getting In Touch With Your Inner Bitch is the ultimate self-help book.

Includes:
Cartoons
The Power Library
and much more . . .

Based on the
***Hysteria* Magazine**
article that generated
tons of press!

"You only start being called bitch when you become successful."
Judith Regan

"I'm tough, ambitious, and I know exactly what I want. If that makes me a bitch, okay."
Madonna

"There's is a bitch in every good cook."
Georgia O'Keefe

There is and integral, powerful part of each of us which is going unrecognized.
It is the Inner Bitch. Don't even pretend you don't know what I'm talking about.
The Inner Bitch is the Bette Davis in each of us, walking around with a cigarette in one hand,
a martini in the other, calling a dump a dump.
The Inner bitch calls it as she sees it.

*T*his is the end of Toxic Niceness as we know it.

collecting

How to Dominate Tag Sales

When negotiations fail, use force

TAG SALES HAVE BEEN AN IMPORTANT PART OF MY LIFE SINCE MY FORMATIVE YEARS in New Jersey. By the time most other girls were smoking cigarettes in the bathrooms and flunking Home Ec, I was busy furnishing my room at home with doo-doo from other people's attics and garages. Quickly, I discovered that you can find everything you need for a perfect existence — linens, antique glassware, glue guns — at these delightfully tacky affairs.

As in life, position is everything at tag sales, which is why I begin preparing well in advance. Shortly after dusk, and once we've located the tag sale site, my staff sets up my tent, outfitting it with a portable stove, Adirondacks-style table and chairs, and provisions and campware for 200 to 300. Then, I dispatch two or three of them to the front door to begin the long wait for the sale to begin the next morning at 9:00.

Should the owner venture out earlier, say to walk the dog or fetch the paper, I serve up a light breakfast of freshly roasted and brewed coffee, orange juice from trees grown in my greenhouse and muffins baked on-site. Later, while the other tag-salers are lining up in front of the tent, my people are well on their way to snatching up every deal and steal in the place.

Being first at the door is only half the battle at some tag sales, however. Occasionally, an aggressive housewife, savvy buyer or greedy home owner will put my staff to the test. That's when I step in.

I have found several simple negotiating tactics to be quite effective in most competitive tag sale situations. For openers, a direct inquiry, spoken clearly and loudly, disarms most sellers: "Excuse me, but you want HOW MUCH for this piece of junk?" is a favorite. When that fails, a few faux cracks applied with a charcoal eye pencil to that amusing set of Flintstone jelly-jar glasses can cause a dramatic reduction in the asking price and an instant sale.

But in other instances, stronger negotiating tactics must be employed. I prefer the police wristlock *(shown on the cover)* to the headlock shown in the photographs *(right)* since the former disables the opponent for several hours after the purchase. Other situations demand still stronger response.

I have had to use my stun gun on only two occasions — both times, I'm happy to report, with unqualified success. Once, I was forced to repel a bid from a determined shopper who otherwise would surely have beaten one of my assistants to a handsome J. Edgar Hoover vanity set. The second time? My attorneys have advised me not to discuss the incident in detail, but I can tell you that it involved some 19th-century French tub tiles and that Bob Vila learned a painful lesson that day.

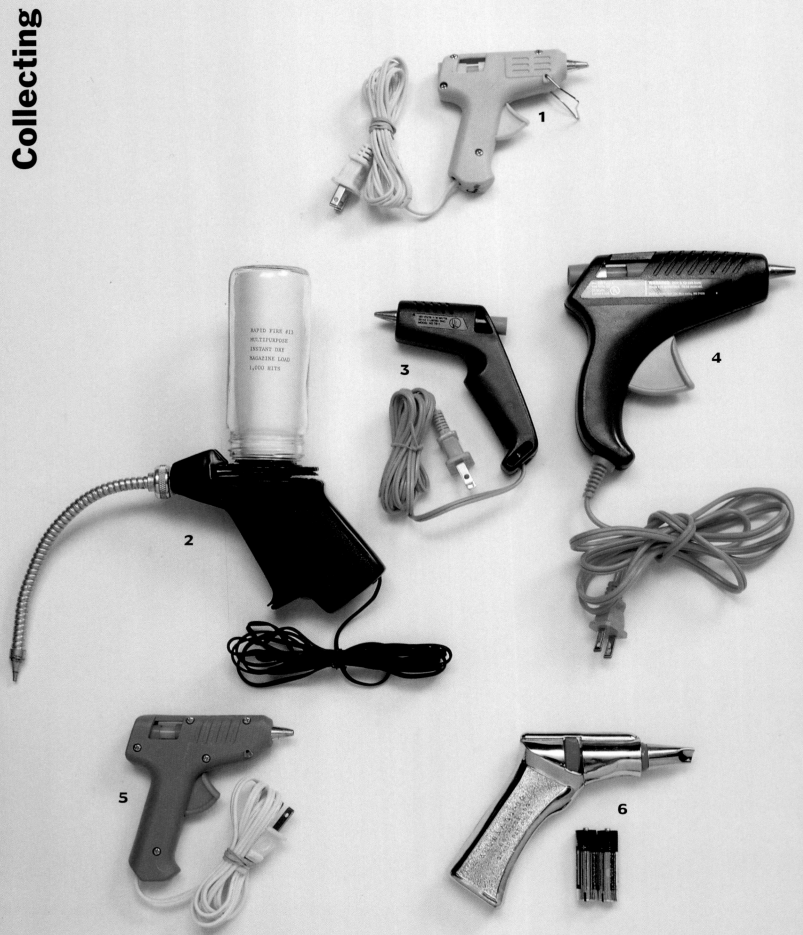

RAPID FIRE #13
MULTIPURPOSE
INSTANT DRY
MAGAZINE LOAD
1,000 HITS

Glue Guns

GLUE GUNS OCCUPY A SPECIAL PLACE IN MY LIFE AND CAN BE FOUND IN EVERY ROOM OF MY HOME. I ADMIRE THE SMOOTH FORM, THE FEEL OF THE TRIGGER UNDER MY FINGER AS I CONTROL THE FLOW OF HOT ADHESIVE. I KEEP ONE ON MY NIGHT TABLE. AT LEFT ARE SIX CLASSIC GLUE GUNS FROM MY PRIVATE COLLECTION. WHEN I NO LONGER NEED THEM, THEY WILL BE BEQUEATHED TO THE STEWSKI RARE GLUE MUSEUM & RESEARCH LIBRARY AT THE UNIVERSITY OF CRAKOW.

1. Hamimoto Hummingbird. As its name implies, this little gem, made on the Pacific Rim, is light, quick and accurate. The Hummingbird can easily be carried in an opera purse and its battery powered capabilities allow it to be used for remote, on-the-spot work. Once, on a flight to Paris, I was summoned to the cockpit when a balky, cracked, throttle handle was jeopardizing the safety of the passengers and crew. My Hummingbird performed its magic and we landed safely at Orly in time for croissants.

2. Bindorff Magnum 44. When it's time to call in the heavy artillery, there is only one gun in town. This powerhouse from the folks that brought you the famous "Longbarrel 38," is the only piece on the market that has a high power, remote turbo pump located at the actual glue reservoir. It's capable of laying down a 3/4-inch bead of pre-mixed epoxy at the rate of 16 feet per minute! Once, in an emergency, I held up the entire north side of my Neutering Barn by gluing the lateral support truss to a conveniently placed oak tree.

3. Allegro Piccolo. This timeless design from Italy, has long been my standby when my artistic reputation is on the line. Its absolute consistency of temperature and feed speed allow complete confidence when working on an important piece. It is the only gun available to the general public that has a selection of tips suitable for fine filigree work. This is the gun I rely on for microscopic projects such as DNA splicing and the like.

4. Mac Pilgrim. This gun, designed by famed New England-crafts guru DeWinter MacKenzie, features a 30,000-watt heating coil — by far the hottest of any modern gun. This tremendous heat causes the glue to thin-out to water-like consistency. Great for taxidermy or ornamental dental work.

5. Macro-Tec Online GDS: Here is the future of glue guns. The Macro-Tec has a wireless data transmission module that monitors heat and glue reservoir levels, then broadcasts the data to a central hub in Kansas. The information is processed on a CRAY 4000 super computer and relayed to the glue supply warehouse in Encinada while a signal is simultaneously sent to Federal Express. At this point, Macro-Tec's GDS, (Glue Delivery System) takes over and at the exact moment the last drop of glue spurts out of your tip, the FEDEX truck will pull up with a new, pre-warmed batch.

6. Franklin Air Drive "Competition Model". This is the gun I use when speed is of the essence. My Franklin helped me to win the J. Paul Getty Speed Restoration Competition seven years in a row. Capable of 60-ft.-per-minute bursts, the Franklin, can really cover some ground. This is a highly specialized tool that should only be used in competition situations due to its finicky nature.

is Martha Stuart **Living?**

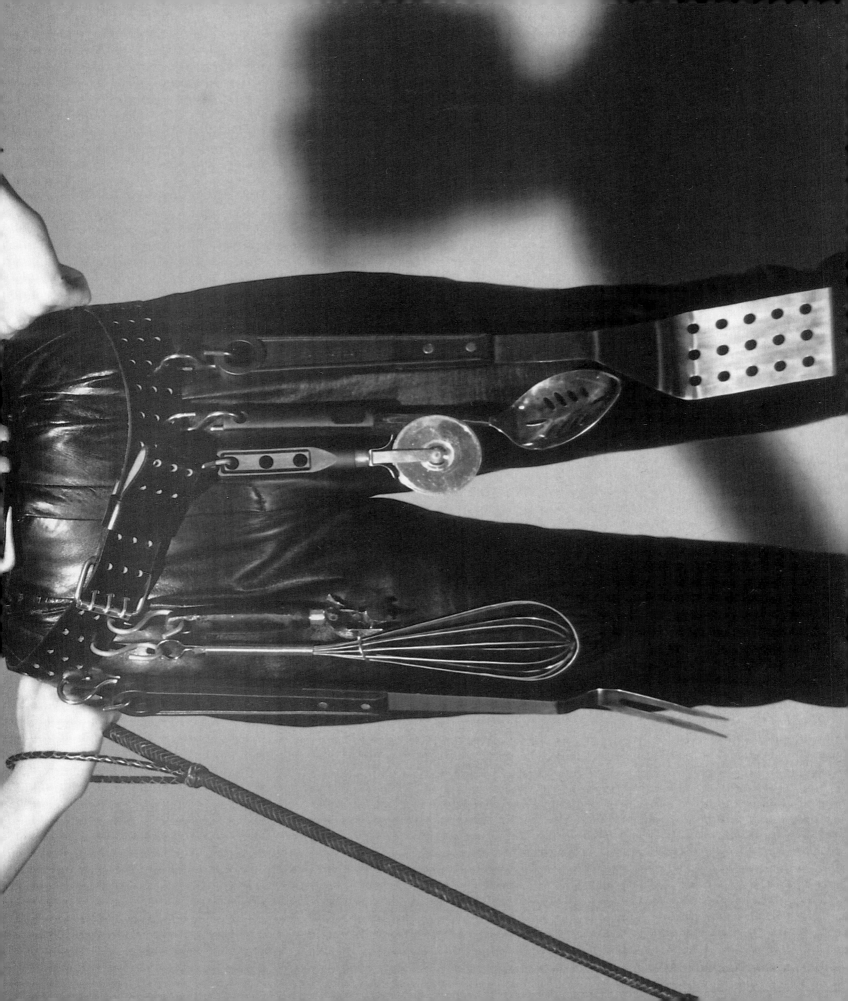

holidays

Pruning sheers and a hot glue gun were all
it took to re-engineer this imperfect
Douglas Fir into a perfect Christmas tree.

THIS IS THE SEASON WE'VE WAITED ALL YEAR FOR. IT IS A TIME TO RELAX, TO RECEIVE FAMILY MEMBERS, TO ENTERTAIN DEAR FRIENDS. IT IS ALSO THE IDEAL TIME TO DEMONSTRATE OUR ABSOLUTE SUPERIORITY IN EVERY ASPECT OF KITCHEN AND HOME.

A Christmas Ham

NO HOLIDAY DINNER IS COMPLETE WITHOUT THE PRESENCE OF A MAGNIFICENT BAKED HAM IN THE CENTER OF THE TABLE, GLISTENING WITH a sugared glaze and scored in a perfect criss-crossed pattern.

The preparation of a 30-pound baked ham is not a task to be taken lightly. In order to realize all its marvelous possibilities, one must become a porcine student of sorts, intimate with the ham's nature, its lineage and character, and the myriad details necessary to achieve perfection in its preparation.

As in all things, it is imperative that you begin well. Establish a close relationship with your butcher, visiting his shop frequently and gaining his respect by proving your knowledge of the meats of the world. Be genteel but also assertive, for you must communicate to him your desire, your deep need, for a superior ham. You must get exactly what you want. Nothing less will do. Ever.

The most critical step in preparing a ham for the holidays, of course, is scoring the top in a classic criss-cross pattern. While taste means something, how things look is infinitely more important. An imperfectly-scored ham simply cannot be served.

I don't expect any sidedish to stand up to one of my hams, so I usually prepare a simple Terrine du Remulade au Pouligny *(see "Recipes")*. Then it is time to sit down and help my guests understand.

Photo: Seth Goltzer

Here is how I prepare my ham:

1. I find that massaging the meat for 40-50-minutes before it goes into the oven helps the ham relinquish any resistance it may have to being cooked.

2. Now align the ham with a reliable fixed point, such as magnetic north, making sure your transit or other measuring instrument has been recently serviced and accurately adjusted.

3. Correct clove placement is absolutely essential to perfect criss-crossing.

Position the cloves one inch apart at 1-5/16ths-of-an-inch intervals, so that they form uniform lines both vertically and diagonally.

4. For excruciatingly straight lines, I rely on a grid pattern based on geo-stationary satellite positions I regularly receive from a friend at NASA. If you should lack this resource, however, a professional compass will have to do.

5. After trimming away the fat to an equal thickness of exactly 3/8ths of an inch all around the ham, take a dangerously sharp knife or new Xacto blade and scribe the surface from northeast to southwest, making incisions 3/32nds-of-an-inch deep. Then work from southeast to northwest in the same manner.

6. For a quick, traditional glaze, try floating a quarter cup of bee pollen on a mixture of sweated wheat grass and clover wine, then gently baste (I use a Windsor & Newton #14 Sable watercolor brush). Preheat the oven to 145 degrees and, basting every half-hour, cook overnight.

Photo: Culver Pictures, Inc.

Photo: Christopher Little/Outline

From time to time, even I feel the need to use an extra person or two to help cook meals and serve guests. Above, a few members of my cooking and catering crew happily prepare a last minute lunch in the auxiliary industrial kitchen behind my Connecticut home. Note the overflow from my copper pot and pan collection on the racks over their heads.

I occasionally hire this woman, shown at left, when sheer volume of food, rather than quality or style, is required. I also use her to test some of my new recipes and clean up around the kitchen before a magazine shoot or televised show.

Spur-of-the-moment gatherings and meals are among my favorites, providing a sponaneity that's unachievable at elaborate parties. But they naturally leave no time for planning or shopping. You must simply throw together wahtever odds and ends you have in the pantries, refrigerators and gardens (above), and hope for the best. Impromptu parties also some-times mean more guests than there are seats at the table. When that happened recently, I expanded the dining room to accommodate an extra 80 people (right).

Dinner Party

You can pour your very soul into the food and the floral arrangements. You can hire a harpist and the finest help. None of that will matter if the guests aren't right.

Try thinking of your holiday party as a fruitcake, with the guest list as the recipe: your closest friends as the eggs, butter and flour that make up the batter; and the models, celebrities and others you'd like to be your friends as the

CONTINUED ON PAGE 42

I love social inter-
course, but at a test
dinner, I'm all busi-
ness. I expect test
guests to really sing
for their supper with
articulate, educated
opinions on every-
thing from the humidi-
ty in the room to the
PH factor of the
wine. I try to get
updates about every
10-15 minutes during
the course of the
evening.

Anything goes as far as the dinner financials are concerned. After all, with a test dinner it's strictly business, nothing personal. I normally factor in my general overhead as well as a **150%** surcharge that goes directly to my **R&D** costs.

candied fruits, nuts, brandy and spices. Remember, though, that a good fruitcake should have only enough batter to bind the fruits and nuts together.

Now go through the cupboard that is your rolodex and ask yourself what kind of fruitcake you could best serve. Sweet and simple? Then you must encourage your guests to bring their children, preferably wearing velvet and already fed and sedated. Strong and intoxi-

Eric Robert/SIGMA

When this guest, a little-regarded director shown left hiding behind the drapery, died suddenly after dinner, I turned what might have been an entertaining disaster into a decorating coup by building a coffin of pine boards in my shop and lining it with a wonderful chintz from the '40s.

cating? Go heavy on desperate singles, euphoric divorcees and loud-mouthed gossips who can hold their liquor. Flaky and nutty? Stick with designers and artists. Classic? Better invite the professional couple with good taste and tweedy clothes from down the street.

Always keep in mind that a guest list isn't a wish list. It is a shopping list of the people you can reasonably expect to respond to your invitation, including those slightly but not totally out of your league (actually, I'm only guessing that's what happens, since no one has ever turned down one of my invitations). In other words, unless your publicist knows mine, don't obsess about how to get me to come to your home.

Since this is also the busiest time of the year for me, amidst the hubbub, I like to relax by throwing an impromptu dinner for 800 or so on a weekday night before the holiday entertaining begins in earnest.

Actually, I must admit to a serious error in planning this year's warmup Christmas party. In setting the table the morning of the party, I discovered that the dining

The guinea-subjects I invite are generally people articulate enough to form an opinion but not important enough for their opinions to carry weight with anyone else. In using a focus group of this type, it is wise to remember not to be constrained by moral, ethical or religious standards of any kind. In other words, feel free to try anything at all.

For the small dinner party I hosted two nights before my annual Christmas buffet for 800, I invited the editorial staff of "Chutzpa!" Magazine up from Manhattan to sample several new dishes assembled entirely from the woods, fields and beaches surrounding my Connecticut, Vermont and East Hampton homes (see "What To Have For Dinner"). I did not reveal the ingredients beforehand, nor the nature of the party itself.

Since even affairs such as this can be quite expensive, I decided with this party to begin charging guests for dinner. This ingenious touch accomplishes two things: it tows the bottom line and it keeps the test-group participants from confusing themselves with my real guests.

Occasionally test guests may have a mild reaction at check time. I pay this absolutely no mind. There are literally thousands of people who would give anything just to sit at my table.

room of my Connecticut home was not big enough to accommodate all the guests I'd invited. The solution occurred to me immediately: Expand the dining room and dining room table. So as soon as it was light outside, I roused the in-house carpentry crew and had them knock out the back wall of the room, then add another 40 feet of space.

That evening, as guests began filling up the house, I noticed several women looking quizzically about the room, trying their damnedest to figure out what was new, what different. I watched them from the doorway, and snickered.

Substance counts for something in life, but I have learned over the years that appearance counts for much more. As long as the food, kitchen, table, home and life look good, they are good.

Even so, before a party of any significance, I always run a controlled test of new recipes.

Relatives

IT IS ALWAYS A GREAT SURPRISE WHEN RELATIVES SHOW UP UNANNOUNCED

AT ONE OF MY HOMES. AND WHILE FOR MANY YEARS I'VE USED MODELS TO POSE AS

FAMILY MEMBERS FOR THE PARTIES I PHOTOGRAPH AND VIDEOTAPE,

MY ACTUAL RELATIVES CONTINUE TO APPEAR FOR HOLIDAYS AND ODD WEEKENDS THROUGHOUT THE YEAR IN THE OLD-WORLD TRADITION OF WANDERING AND IMPOSING. CAMPED OUT IN THE FIELDS WITHIN SIGHT OF THE KITCHEN, THEY BEGIN ARRIVING LATE THURSDAY NIGHT AND REMAIN, CONSTRUCTING YURT-LIKE DWELLINGS AND SINGING SONGS OR LAMENTATIONS, UNTIL THE LAST OF THE "GUESTS" HAVE RETURNED TO THEIR HOMES AND THE LEFT-OVER FOOD HAS BEEN DEPOSITED IN THE TRASH CANS, ONLY THEN DO THEY APPROACH THE MAIN HOUSE. ONE OF THE JOYS OF HAVING MY RELATIVES VISIT, HOWEVER, IS WATCHING THEM PREPARE A TRADITIONAL FAMILY MEAL WE SIMPLY CALLED "TYBR RUDSKI," OR "SMOLDERING TUBERS." BELOW IS THE ORIGINAL RECIPE, AS PRESERVED ON AN INDEX CARD BY MY GRANDMOTHER SOPHIE:

Smoldering Tubers

- First, scrounging with bare red hands in a muddy field on a cold fall or spring day, remove whatever potatoes, beets, onions and other rhizomes that were missed during harvest.
- Once most, but not all, of the dirt has been scraped away with a stick or tongue depressor, wrap the tubers in schmattas and soak overnight in vodka.
- Bury the tubers in a smokey fire of kindling from used building materials, then cook until a fork's tines sink in and bend without breaking.
- Drizzle with rainwater and serve luke-warm but still smoldering.

THE DISTINCTIVE AROMA OF THIS BASIC COUNTRY DISH HANGS IN THE AIR LONG AFTER I'VE CHANGED ADDRESSES.

R. Custom Fine Boots

You can have ANY STYLE of boots, shoes, felt hats or leather clothing custom made to your EXACT design & size!

Our background as saddlemakers gives us the tools and skills to produce EXACTLY WHAT YOU WANT IN LEATHER OR SUEDE.

Are you size 16-EEEEE or 4-AAAAA?   Size 62-Tall X-X-X-X-Wide Leg - X-X-X-X-Skinny? We can fit them all.

You will get great looking boots or leathers that fit *you* perfectly!

In a hurry? Try our RUSH service.

Or, choose from our HUGE, in-stock collection including hard-to-fit/hard-to-find sizes, styles & colors.

Please come in or call 203-227-6272 to order by phone. Ask for Bobby, Chris or Ron

The TACK ROOM
153 Post Road East · Westport, CT
(Across from the Post Office)
(203) 227-6272 · Fax: 227-8610

KIDS KORRAL

Frock coat with bone trim and matching bone boots & bag.

Childs vests, hats & boots start as small as size infants size "6 months."

Put your child's feet in our hands! Our "GROWING LINER" system gives your child a perfect fit — *and room to grow!* This system is FREE on any children's boots.

★ ★
Your genuine leather children's boots are treated for FREE to keep your kids feet warm & dry.
★ ★

H

Enjoy the Comfort and Durability
of the Finest Leather and Country Clothing

Today with all of the "faux" country western brands out there, it's easy to purchase leather clothing that is country styled — but not really country rugged. All of the leather clothing and boots you find at our shop are country rugged. Built to the standard you would expect from Fairfield County's oldest riding and leather clothing shop. While you may not be going horseback riding with our great looking leather coats and boots, we build every item as if you were! Of course, in addition to our huge selection, any item you desire can be custom made-to-order in your choice of leathers, colors and sizes.

★ ★

MY GUARANTEE TO YOU!

If *anytime* you feel your Tack Room boots or leathers haven't given you the COMFORT & DURABILITY you deserve — Bring them back and we will repair or replace them FREE!

Since 1962 we have stood for the finest quality and value. Value to us doesn't just mean durability — we know our products are built to last; it includes COMFORT!

This means that *even if you have worn your boots, we will take them back and repair or replace them as needed to make sure you are COMFORTABLE!!!*

Ronald S. Friedson
President

"WE GUARANTEE YOUR COMFORT,
FOR AS LONG AS YOU OWN YOUR BOOTS!"

★ ★

Larry Mahan
HANDCRAFTED IN EL PASO, TX

L

100's of belts in stock for men, women & children!

K

Lucchese
SINCE 1883

M

Camp Martha

A DISCIPLINARY CRAFTS CAMP FOR CHILDREN

W hat better way to instill life-correcting lessons about productive behavior than by teaching children crafts? At Camp Martha, children who are aggressive, domineering, anal-compulsive or alarming overachievers learn how to channel those traits into crafts, crops and baked goods that sell. Under the firm guidance of Martha Stuart and her staff, your child will produce an MDQ (minimum daily quota) of 100 units a week during the Christmas, Easter or summer vacation.

Send today for my color brochure, application, gift catalog and price list.

These "dunce-cap" cookies, produced by crafts-challenged campers, brought $12 each at the camp store.

the recipes

Calamari Gelato

SERVES 2

2   fresh warm water squid about 6 Oz. each

1/2   Cup heavy cream

1/2   Cup Sweet & Low

1. Clean and eviscerate squid under fresh water, saving ink pouch as well as two sets of tentacles for presentation.

2. Heat heavy cream and Sweet & Low to a gently rolling boil.

3. Smash squid parts by hand until smooth. Add enough squid ink to change color to that of grey flannel.

4. Combine ingredients and stir briskly until most of the fish smell disappears.

5. Freeze

Serving Suggestion:

Put one or two scoops in a fluted ice cream dish. Place tentacles on Gelato and top with a sprig of mint. Wait for complIments.

Simple Marmalade

SERVES 6

4   white cardamom pods (grown in July)

1   teaspoon yellow mustard seeds (grown in early July)

2   teaspoon extra,extra,extra virgin canola oil (bought in late June)

1/64 teaspoon crushed red pepper skins

4   large elephant garlic cloves peeled and lightly smashed with a ball peen hammer

11   sun-dried tomatoes

1   yellow pepper

1   red pepper

1   green pepper

1   blue pepper

1   poblano pepper

1   red onion

1   white onion

1   yellow onion

1   beefsteak tomato

1   cherry tomato

1   plum tomato

1   teaspoon, hand evaporated sea salt.

1. Chop ingredients by hand for three hours or until very finely diced. Serve on toasted 90-grain bread rounds.

Hunters' Stew

SERVES 600

In the old country when the men went hunting, the women would bring a great pot of stew out to the fields where they would cook it over a roaring fire. While not exactly a low fart dish, this will satisfy the appetite of even the most savage hunter.

24	pounds fresh sauerkraut
1	pound bacon, cut into tiny slabs
1	pound boneless lamb, cut into 1/2 inch pieces
1	pound boneless pork, cut into 3/4 inch pieces
1	pound boneless, round eye beef, cut into 1 inch pieces
1	pound goose liver
1	pound kielbasa
1	pound lard
1	pound salt
1	pound suet
5	pounds butter
3	pounds fatback

1. Combine ingredients in a 55 gallon oil drum. Heat over a fire made from one pine tree. Serve on flat rocks.

90-Grain Bread

SERVES 2

This is simply the best, most nutritious, as well as politically-correct, bread recipe I have ever come across.

6	cups 90-grain flour (see #1)
2	cups homemade water
1	teaspoon homemade baking soda
1	teaspoon homemade sugar

1. Drop by the U.S. Department of Agriculture and pick up a selection of grain seeds from English-speaking, democratic countries. At this point, there are about 101 left. Pick out the most handsome seeds. You will find 90.
2. Plant in the spring.
3. Harvest in the fall.
4. Separate the wheat from the chaff and grind. I find that nothing beats a good old-fashioned windmill for this purpose. I own one. If you don't, any millstones you have will do.
5. Combine ingredients to form dough. Alternately kneed and let rise every hour for one day. There's no time for sleeping on this one!
6. Form loaf into an interesting shape. I get the most compliments on my combination Challa Braid/DNA Double-Helix look.
7. Bake in a clay or brick oven. I own one. If you don't, any industrial proofing, or professional baker's oven will do.
8. Let cool for 47 seconds. Serve warm on a White Ash bread board with homemade butter.

Four Season Poached Egg

SERVES 1

This wonderful, 12-month folk recipe was handed down to me by my great great Uncle Yorgi and is sure to please.

Winter:

Out you go to the chicken run, on the morn of January one;

Grab one poulets masterpiece, check for every known disease; Bring it in, with bees wax paint it. Just make sure the wax ain't tainted;

With mud and burlap, wrap that thing. Store it under buttermilk, wait for spring.

Spring:

May one comes with cows-a-moo'in, there's one thing you must be doin';

Pull that orb from its milky rest, shine with silk till you've done your best;

Find a rocky promontory, set that egg in old sol's glory;

Wait four months until the day, your egg's shadow has gone away.

Summer:

Down to the pond, to the brook, to the stream, icy water makes a white egg gleam;

Bury under moss with a cat's hairball, top with yogurt and wait for Fall.

Fall:

When Fall begins, the leaves-a-crunchin', your egg is almost set for munchin';

Poach it now but just remember, you can't eat that egg 'till late December.

CHRISTOPHER PEACOCK
FURNITURE *for the* KITCHEN

television

PROGRAM GUIDE

The show is designed for those who missed features in the magazine, chapters in the books, segments on the home videos, readings on audio tapes and CDs, articles about me in national magazines and newspapers, access to me on Internet and CompuServe, preparations on morning network television, appearances on other network or cable tv programs, demonstrations in Kmart outlets, or lectures or seminars in person. If you miss these episodes, watch for the forthcoming Broadway musical & feature film.

DECEMBER 23-25 EPISODE 91

Holidays: Constructing A Gingerbread Replica of Windsor Castle

Cooking: Grilling with Cats

Decorating: Competitive Gilding

Things: Insomnia

Gingerbread Castle

MATERIALS
Large work area
1/2-ton gingerbread mix
750 tubes of royal icing
200-lbs. assorted hard candies
Cement-mixing boat & long-handled trowel
Foundation forms
Levels, t-squares & plumb bob
Heat gun
Industrial glue gun
Scaffolding
Architectural plans of Castle

Miniature gingerbread cottages, private homes and historic buildings are fun but also cliches by now. Anyone can make them, and most of my readers have. For a challenge this holiday season, try constructing this exact 1/12th-scale replica of the Royal family's residence outside of London.

1. Combine ingredients into cement boat, adding water from garden hose, and work until the consistency of gruel. In a wheelbarrow, add pebbles, bottle caps and any small, sharp objects to strengthen the mix and dissuade children from eating completed castle. Dump into foundation forms and spread onto industrial cooking sheets or directly onto floor. Flatten with a garden roller or street-paving Rollmaster.
2. Following plans, trace wall sections and make cutouts for doors, windows, battlements, etc.
3. Apply heat gun to surfaces until baked dry (time: 14 days)
4. After erecting pipe scaffolding, set block & tackle and raise and swing panels into place. Glue at edges and cover seams with icing.
5. Glue hard candies in place for door handles, hinges, knockers, etc. Use enough glue so children will be unable to remove.

Cooking With Cats

Cat steaks are prized throughout the Far East and especially Mexico where, when cooked over mesquite on, say, a '53 Chevy grille, even the scroungiest of alley cat can taste like fowl. After skinning and quartering, cut into stirp steaks and rinse with a good mescal. Heat grille over mesquite bricquettes and
arrange catmeat in an interesting way. Drink rest of the mescal. Sing "Mamasita, donde esta Santa Claus?" over and over. Pass out before dinner is served.

Insomnia Workshop

It is little wonder housewives get so little accomplished. They spend too much time sleeping and not enough time working. But thanks to insomnia (which I have had since childhood), I've created an entire second workshift in life. Viewers will be encouraged to developed this most useful homekeeping tool.

FUTURE SHOWS

Episode 97

Cooking: Impromptu Bouillabaisse for 700

Things: Flavored Colonic Purges

Grounds: Building a Neutering Shed

WHAT TO HAVE FOR
dinner

recollecting

A Garden State of Mind

by Martha Stuart

MORE AND MORE THESE DAYS, I FIND MYSELF WANDERING OVER TO THE TRAILER HOME PARKED at the rear of my Connecticut estate for when my mother and sisters visit. Here, late at night, I've been decorating the interior and exterior with the household objects of my childhood: concrete statues of deer and the Seven Dwarfs placed around the tiny front yard; cut-glass dishes from Woolworth's filled with red Chuckles and set out on top of the coffee table or color TV; plastic covers on the armchairs and sofas; anything painted on velvet.

Twenty years on the analyst's couch (which I recently re-covered) may have helped me manage my compulsion to gild everything in sight, but they haven't eradicated my roots. Last night, after decorating until well past midnight, I fell asleep on the Castro convertible out in the trailer and dreamed the following dream:

I am standing in what appears to be a parking lot next to a Dairy Queen or A&W Root Beer drive-in. There are a lot of Harleys and cars with bright, candy-apple red paint jobs. I am fat. My white rabbit fur bomber jacket has mustard stains on it. My jeans have been stone-washed and have zippers at the ankles. I feel my hair. It is loaded with spray. I have the strange sensation that I know the Jersey shore.

Now I am on line in a White Castle. From somewhere I can hear the strains of "Disco Inferno." I am very fat, and also very hungry. I want to order 20 cheeseburgers and cram all 20 of those little suckers in my mouth at once. As I move up toward the cash register, the guy behind me starts rubbing himself against my buttocks. I become aroused.

Now I am in a bedroom. I am wearing fuzzy pink slippers and lying on a bed that is huge and round and covered with an orange-and-black crushed velvet bedspread. On the walls are oil paintings of dogs playing poker, the sight of which makes my eyes all misty. There is also a poster of Jon Bon Jovi. I like Jon Bon, a lot. I

also realize that there is a skinny man with a gold tooth standing at the foot of the bed smiling at me. I like him, too. I am really fat now. I start to wake up.

As terrifying as this dream was, I woke up feeling oddly at home and began fantasizing about what my life might have been like had I stayed in New Jersey.

I'd live in a ranch house with plastic flowers in the window boxes and green cement for a lawn. I'd pop TV dinners in the micro when friends came over for dinner, and do whatever I wanted without the entire country watching to see if I screw up. I'd sleep late, bowl on a team, have dates with guys named Fast Eddie and Ralph and Joe. I'd be free, I'd be me, I'd be happy.

Of course, I'd probably also be enormously fat, poor, imperfect, unfamous and, well, still from New Jersey.

Gott   gild.

Also, do you have any ideas on how I can get marshmallow pieces to float in jello?
— G. Steinem
New York City

Dear Steinem:
Fend for yourself, babe.

Dear Martha:

With winter approaching, I'm wondering if there is some way I can induce my eaves to produce icicles. The effect I am after is the filigree ice resembling the very tips of Christmas trees. Any assistance you can offer will be greatly appreciated.
— Yours very sincerely,
Bitsy Price-Jones
Hobe Sound, Florida

Dear Bitsy:
What a charming note. On the issue of icicles, an early obstacle to overcome is the fact that you live in Florida. I say `obstacle' because nothing is impossible and, in fact, after speaking with my brother Harold, and upon a little experimentation, I've found that the solution is to build a series of fiberglass spouts along the gutterline. Once in place, install a refrigeration unit in the attic. Good luck, and do let me know how it turns out.

Dear Martha Stuart:

I seen you at the Kmart over in Dime Box the other day while shopping for a new dress shirt and string tie for Duane. As a mother of six children and wife, a course, to him, which is no picnic believe me, I hardly have time to fart before dinner, much less sew napkins like you were making there in the store. I just thought you should know.
— Bonnie Wells
Covalis, Texas

Dear Bonnie:
Don't be ridiculous. No one is married to a man named Duane.

Dear Martha:

As a recent graduate of the Ambassador Training Institute (AIU), I was particularly interested in the article entitled "Economical Fish Entreés for Third-World Revolutionaries" that appeared in your last issue.

Using your methods, I successfully satiated 6,800 members of Iraq's elite Presidential Guard, and believe me, they're tough customers!

Never has the embassy been so alive as when I rolled out the "Grouper En Crouté" on a Sverlovsky-Armed Personnel Carrier. The sights and sounds of the revolution created a dramatic back-drop for the lovely dinner.
— Thanks again
Capt. Chip Marston
Schwingham
(a.k.a. "ShabazzX")

Dear Skank,
Me and the boys down at Swifty's Grill got a bone to pick with you, so to speak. Our wives been readin your rag and gettin some pretty wrongheaded ideas in their brains. We like em the way they were. We like em the way they used to dress before they started wearin all this cotton stuff that costs a G note and what not. We don't even know the name of the crap we're gettin for dinner these days. But you wouldn't understand that would you? You look like you haven't had a decent meal since Frank Sinatra retired. Now I'm as easy goin as the next guy, but I'll be damned if I'm gonna trade in my Ranger bass boat for a set of Tiffany cheese knives.

What I'm gettin around to here is... If you want to go ahead and teach your fancy friends how to spend two days makin a piece of toast, that's hunky- dory. Just keep your quiche outa my mailbox.
— I remain,
BIG AL
Queens

Dear Martha:

I am considering going into the business of telling other women what to do in their homes and would like to know how many death threats you receive a month.
— Just Curious
Westport, Connecticut

Dear Curious:
Seven-thousand five-hundred and thirty-seven.

Summer at a Shoreline for the rest of your life.

The Hamptons? The Cape? The Vineyard? The Jersey Shore? Each summer, you face the same decision – "where to take your vacation?"

Why not spend your next vacation at one of the most beautiful Shorelines ever created? Your own.

The beauty and quality of each Shoreline pool reflects a level of experience that has been developed through years of being the leading builder of pools in the Northeast. Since 1969, Shoreline has designed, constructed, main-tained, serviced and restored over 3,000 pools in the area, each of which is unique in its own style, design and setting.

Pools built with Shoreline's quality of materials and workmanship more than 25 years ago continue to provide the same enjoyment and pleasure for their owners that they did the day they were built.

For a lifetime of enjoyment for you and your family, call Shoreline today and make plans to summer at your own Shoreline.

shoreline pools
A Tradition of Quality
288 Valley Road • Cos Cob, CT
203-869-1203

A Shoreline vacation without leaving home.

It's going to be 90 degrees out with 95 per cent humidity… And the closest ocean is more than an hour of bumper to bumper traffic away… And once you get there, it's sure to be wall to wall people…

There is a better way. Take your vacation at your own Shoreline…without ever leaving home.

Dedicated to building swimming pools of only the highest quality, from traditional formal pools to unique free-form presentations, Shoreline will utilize its experi-ence and expertise to effectively integrate patios, spas, decks, rock walls and waterfalls.

From the initial concept to a weekly service program, Shoreline will meet each of your needs. For over 25 years, thousands of satisfied customers have chosen Shoreline to design, construct, restore, and service their pools.

So call today and find out how you can take a Shoreline vacation… right in your own back yard.

shoreline
pools
A Tradition of Quality

288 Valley Road • Cos Cob, CT
203-869-1203

the guide

Items pictured in this issue but not listed are from individuals or organizations who fear attribution

CORRECTION
In the spring issue, I suggested making an infant rattle out of dried belladonna pods and seeds. Actually, my attorneys have advised me that this is the most unsafe type of rattle one could possibly give a baby and, in fact, should be kept well out of reach of children and even some adults.

COVER
Carnival **glass** **Gaylordsville**, *CT tag sale, now part of Martha's antique glass* collection, *$175, from K-mart.*

LETTER
FROM MARTHA
PAGE 4
Dried **flowers**, $165 and $205, from Martha's Good 'N Dead flower shop, *Westport, CT* ; white turtleneck **sweater** $80 *from M. Stuarts, East Hampton, NY.*

THINGS
PAGE 9
Perfectly-stacked **logs** *borrowed from neighbors' woods near Vermont home;* log **table**, $1,295. *from Camp Martha catalog.* **Chicks** (accidentally runover in driveway by a **Range Rover,** $38,000, *from Range Rover of Greenwich,*

CT) available from Chickens Were Us, Bethel, CT.

HOMEKEEPING
PAGE 12
Handmade **brooms,** $90, *from the Camp Martha crafts shop.*

DETAILS
PAGE 17
Porcelain **chamber pot**, $72, *from the In The Bathroom With Martha collection, available at Kmart.* "My Own Private Poland" **bottled water,** $9.95, *distributed by Martha Springs.*

GIFTMAKING
PAGE 24
Cupid stencil, $7, *from Martha's Love Notions (catalog available upon request).* **Vegetables** *from Martha's Country Market, Westport, CT.*

GARDENING
PAGE 18
Map of Martha's Garden **drawing,** $12.50, available from *Is Martha Stuart LIVING magazine.* **Dirt collection**, $6 per sample, *from Martha's World of Dirt, Bridgeport, CT.*

COLLECTING
PAGE 23
Classic **glue guns** *on loan from the Martha Stuart private Glue Gun Collection in the Rare Glue Library & Research Center, University of Crackow.*

CENTERFOLD
PAGE 32
Leather **pants** courtesy of *Martha's Closet, Greenwich Village, New York.* Spanking-new **kitchen utensils**, various prices, *from Pots and Pain, East Village, NYC.*

HOLIDAY
ENTERTAINING
PAGE 45
Christmas **tree (disassembled)**, $100, *from*

Martha's Tree Farm, Putney, VT.
Glue gun, (see under "Collecting"). Perfectly scored **baked ham** & various **scoring devices** *from Stuart Precision Dining, Westport, CT. Dinner guests available for recipe-testing from Chutzpah! Magazine, NY, NY.*

WHAT TO HAVE
FOR DINNER
PAGE 57
Open lawn & woodlands **salad**, $8.50 per serving, and Spicy squid-ink **sorbet**, $6 per cone, *available in the Camp Martha cafeteria.* Free-range **cat steaks**, $129.95 per frozen dozen, *from Marthasita's.*

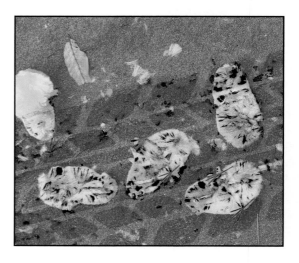

OPEN LAWN & WOODLAND SALAD

WILD CAT STEAKS

CALAMARI GELLATO

PREPARATION SCHEDULE

1. Ride sitdown mower

2. Rake up lawn greens

3. Forage for freebies in woods

4. Hunt cats at town dump

5. Comb beach for washed-up squid

6. Have stylist arrange in appetizing manner.

Above: A hearty outdoors' salad, free for the gathering. This menu was inspired by early fall cleanup around the properties and by my policy of spending as little as possible on dinner guests.

Opposite: Wild cat steaks grill before unsuspecting guests arrive.

Page 55: A tentacle adds a witty garnish to squid-ink gellato; the suction cups keep it in place.